A
TIME OF
BLESSINGS
AND
PEACE

30 Mini-Retreats to Celebrate

the Retirement Years

WILLIAM B. MILLER

**TWENTY-THIRD
PUBLICATIONS**

twentythirdpublications.com

TWENTY-THIRD PUBLICATIONS
977 Hartford Turnpike Unit A
Waterford, CT 06385
(860) 437-3012 or (800) 321-0411
www.twentythirdpublications.com

Copyright © 2023 William B. Miller. All rights reserved. No part of this publication may be reproduced in any manner without prior written permission of the publisher. Write to the Permissions Editor.

Cover photo: stock.adobe.com/Smileus

ISBN: 978-1-62785-778-9
Printed in the U.S.A.

A division of Bayard, Inc.

CONTENTS

Concentrating on Relationship Building

ACKNOWLEDGMENTS

So much goes into writing a book like this. In my case, I have had a great deal of help. I am very grateful to my wife, Marilyn, who located many of the Scripture references found at the end of each chapter. In addition, Marilyn served as a proofreader and a constant source of support to me as I researched and wrote this book. I am very grateful to my good friend Lisa Massello, who found many of the songs that are included at the end of the chapters. I think you will find that spending time with both the Scripture passages and the songs (available on YouTube Music) can be a profound way to pray and meditate. These tools, as well as the thoughts for reflection at the end of each chapter, should prove to be valuable assets for your spiritual nourishment and growth.

I am also grateful to the many friends who contributed stories and wisdom to these pages. I am so very blessed by the presence of each of them in my life. They were also part of the "prayer team." Their prayers and words of encouragement were invaluable.

I thank my editors, Kathy Hendricks and Anne Louise Mahoney, and the entire staff at Twenty-Third Publications for their tireless energy on behalf of this Spirit-led project.

Last but not least, I am grateful to my parents, Orville and Margaret Ann Miller, who, by the grace of God, gave me the foundation in faith, hope, and love to help me become who I am today!

For all of this and so much more I say: Thanks be to God!

INTRODUCTION

As I write tonight, I am living my 74th year. It has been ten years since I stopped working full-time. Since then, I have been actively engaged in volunteer service, spiritual direction training and practice, and developing my skills as an author. At this stage of my life, I have also found myself reflecting often about what I have learned over the years—especially in the realm of spiritual development. I have had help in this pursuit. Esteemed spiritual writers such as Fr. Richard Rohr, Sr. Joan Chittister, Sr. Janet Schaeffler, and Robert Wicks (among others) have helped me find perspective and provided me with some of their hard-won wisdom regarding the process of aging gracefully and growing spiritually in the process. I am most grateful for these mentors.

I am also convinced that I am called to share bits and pieces of their wisdom as well as my own discoveries about what might be called "spirituality in the sunset years." After all, countless research studies have demonstrated that we are capable of intellectual, emotional, and spiritual growth throughout our lives. So, to think of the retirement years only as a time of decline and disorder is a terrible mistake.

In these later years of life, our attitude about aging and about life in general is just as important as it has always been. In *Man's Search for Meaning*, Viktor Frankl writes: "Everything can be taken away from us but one thing: the last of human freedoms—to choose one's attitude in any given set of circumstances." Therefore, let us cultivate an attitude of openness, a willingness to reflect upon the stories of our lives, and use them as opportunities to grow. And let us embrace the stories of others and glean from them the wisdom they provide. In *The Gift of Years*, Joan Chittister describes eloquently the road we are being invited to travel:

This is the period of spiritual reflection, of spiritual renewal in life. Now is the time to ask ourselves what kind of person we have been becoming all these years. And do we like that person? Did we become more honest, more decent, more caring, more merciful....? And if not, what must we be doing about it now?

In his book *After 50*, Robert Wicks describes a profound conversation he had with one of his spiritual mentors as they walked along the Shenandoah River. Out of the blue, his friend and mentor said,

> "I think now may be a good time for you to take your spiritual life more seriously."...What I instantly felt he was trying to tell me was that it was time to leap more freely and deeply into what was truly more important in life. It was time to really:
> - Seek and embrace God at the center of my life;
> - Care for others from a deeper place in my soul; and
> - Nurture my own interior life through creative, new, and simple ways.

In the pages that follow, you will find thirty chapters or reflections. Use them daily for a period of thirty days or space them out over any number of days or weeks. Each reflection contains a short essay plus a question to ponder. Each also includes one or two Scripture references and one or two sacred songs to enrich your prayer time. The reflections, Scripture passages, and/or songs can also be broken open using a *Lectio* method, which gives you the opportunity to go into more depth with the topics, if desired (see chapter 6 for more about the *Lectio* approach). Most important, simply be open to the inspiration of the Holy Spirit, revealed to you in the process.

May the Spirit inspire you and give you peace!

EXPANDING YOUR UNDERSTANDING OF PRAYER

1. Getting to Know You

The title of this chapter comes from the beautiful song written by Rodgers and Hammerstein for the Broadway musical and film *The King and I.*

We will never know all there is to know about our wonderful triune God: Father, Son, and Holy Spirit. However, we can learn many qualities and characteristics by virtue of reflecting upon our faith, sacred Scripture, church history, and the scholarship of numerous excellent teachers and authors.

And, while we can assume that God knows everything about us, God constantly delights in hearing about what we are discovering daily about ourselves, the world around us, and the Divine. As we deepen our relationship with God, we are invited to fall more and more in love.

So, how do we cultivate this special loving relationship with God? The process begins with awareness. Saint Ignatius of Loyola suggested that we must train ourselves to find God in all things: in people, in works of art and in nature, as well as in those places (like a church building) where we customarily think of God.

Many years ago, I attended a marvelous workshop where the instructor hung a series of thirty pictures from various magazines on the walls of the classroom. He asked each of us to find one picture that captured some characteristic of God. There were photographs of people as well as of beautiful landscapes and inanimate objects. One participant chose a picture of an interaction between a woman (possibly a mother) and a child. There was obviously great love and affection being shared. She explained why she chose the picture: "I see love here. God is love."

I have conducted this exercise many times over the years with various age groups. It opens the door to further conversation about the beauty and grandeur of God and the many ways we can be reminded of God's presence in our lives—if we have "eyes to see." Moreover, it is intriguing to observe how two people can pick the very same picture yet see two completely different metaphors for God. Because each person brings her or his own story (set of experiences) to the picture, each has a unique interpretation.

The spiritual writer Paula D'Arcy is fond of saying, "God comes to us disguised as our lives." Indeed, God is as close to us as the air we breathe, always inviting us to enter more deeply into loving relationship. Practicing the virtue of awareness of God takes time and reflection, but the rewards are both inspiring and satisfying. Hopefully, at this stage of our lives, we have more *time to reflect*. I can tell you from personal experience that I have developed a greater appreciation for the presence of the Lord in my life since my retirement, as I strive to put into practice the realization that my Lord is right here, right now—loving me unconditionally.

FOR REFLECTION: *Think about one particular way you have felt God's grandeur within you or in a relationship with another person.*

FOR READING: *John 3:16, Philippians 1:6*

FOR LISTENING: *"Love Broke Through" (Toby Mac);*
"Goodness of God" (Ce Ce Winans)

2. Lessons from Saint Ignatius

As a young soldier, Saint Ignatius Loyola had a powerful spiritual awakening while recovering from a severe wound that he suffered during a battle. While the injury and surgery were very painful, the long recovery process presented him with significant time to grow in his relationship with God. In fact, it was during this period that he resolved to found a religious order (the Society of Jesus, or Jesuits) and pledged to devote the remainder of his life to prayer, study, writing, and the administration of the Jesuits. Retirement can be a bit like a recovery process as one recovers from a life lived at a hectic pace. Consider taking a little time now to become more familiar with Ignatian spirituality.

Ignatian spirituality is built on the premise that the world and everything in it are part of God's magnificent creation. Therefore, the world is good. In fact, Ignatius insists: "All the things in this world are gifts of God, created for us, to be the means by which we can come to know him better, love him more surely and serve him more faithfully."

So it is that we can look at a bee pollinating a flower, a spider weaving an intricate web, and a robin building a nest as examples of the grandeur of God. Likewise, we can appreciate the intimacy of a mother who holds her child to her breast, a conductor who directs an orchestra, and an architect who designs an incredible building—the list goes on and on—and see the hand of God in all of these extraordinary experiences.

Through the centuries, many books have been written about Ignatius, his practices, and his prayer styles. His influence on Christian spirituality has been and continues to be profound! Here are two of the forms of prayer he created and made popular through his teaching:

The Examen: This is slightly different from the examination of conscience, which is often used before celebrating the Sacrament of Reconciliation. In the Examen, we mentally review the events of the day to see where the goodness of God was particularly present or where we failed to appreciate it and act upon it.

Pope John XXIII, the initiator of the Second Vatican Council, found this practice so effective and important that he prayed it twice a day: once at lunchtime and once at bedtime. He did not want to miss a single important detail of his day, so he "backed up" his memory (like a computer) twice a day.

Another centuries-old (and still popular) Ignatian prayer technique is gospel contemplation. In this practice, we use our senses in an imaginative way to reflect upon a gospel passage, making it come alive. We enter into the scene and live there for a few minutes, becoming a character in the story—at times even interacting with other characters.

Details on both of these popular prayer practices, as well as other interesting information about Saint Ignatius and the Jesuits, can be found at www.ignatianspirituality.com. Explore and enjoy!

FOR REFLECTION: *Visit the website listed above and learn a bit more about Ignatian spirituality. Take a cue from Saint Ignatius and try out one of his prayer techniques.*

FOR READING: *Genesis 1:31*

FOR LISTENING: *"Holy Ground" (John Michael Talbot); " Thy Word" (Amy Grant)*

3. Trust—Surrender—Patience

For many of us, the concept of spiritual surrender is one of the least understood and most difficult to practice of all spiritual principles. This is due, in part, to the very human tendency to want to have control over everything that affects our lives.

According to *Webster's New World College Dictionary* (fourth edition), the most common definition of surrender, and the one that is generally implied in a secular (non-spiritual) context, is "to give up possession of or power over; yield to another on demand or compulsion." The *spiritual definition* of surrender is more closely represented by the second definition found in that dictionary: "to give up claim to; give over or yield, esp. voluntarily, as in favor of another."

There is a vitally important distinction between these two legitimate definitions of surrender. The first is used in adversarial situations such as contests, battles, or wars. One of the two parties has been overwhelmed. They have lost the contest and must give up. On the other hand, the definition that applies to spiritual surrender means that one party recognizes the right and responsibility of the other party to exercise control over the situation.

As we move into our retirement years, it is important to understand, appreciate, and apply the principle of spiritual surrender. Otherwise, we risk a twilight of anxiety and frustration. And to be successful at surrender, we must also apply the virtues of trust and patience.

A story from a good friend of mine illustrates these three principles working together. Early in her career, working for a not-for-profit food distribution organization, Cara would attend an annual national conference where chapters of her organization would meet to network and plan strategies for making the organization more effective. Cara was bright and energetic and felt that she would be a great addition to the national board of directors. She considered running for the board, but colleagues suggested that she was not well known by the general membership and might lack the experience necessary for such a position. She was disappointed but decided not to run.

Cara stayed with the organization for many years, contributing to its success in significant ways. As she was approaching the end of her career, the time for election of new board members came around once again. To her great surprise, she received a call from a member of the nominating committee asking her if she would consider running for president of the board.

She thought her chance at such a position had passed years earlier. After reflection, prayer, and conversations with respected colleagues, she decided to run. She and the other members of her slate worked hard, worked smart, and won the election. In retrospect, she realized that when she trusted the Lord enough to give God her leadership dream and had gone about her day-to-day responsibilities to the organization with integrity, professionalism, and patience, she eventually received an opportunity to seek a leadership position above and beyond what she had anticipated.

Being able to know when to let go of the need to control and simply fall into God's loving embrace is perhaps the true meaning of the principle of spiritual surrender.

FOR REFLECTION: *Have you ever tried to give something to God during your prayer time? If so, were you able to leave it with God, or did you keep taking it back?*

FOR READING: *Isaiah 26:4; Colossians 1:9–11*

FOR LISTENING: *"Thy Will" (Hillary Scott and The Scott Family); "Take Lord, Receive" (St. Louis Jesuits); "Even If" (Mercy Me)*

4. The Life-changing Attitude of Gratitude

As retirees, at this time in our lives we have had the opportunities to experience much of what life has to offer in terms of blessings, struggles, joy, suffering, and growth. Sr. Janet Schaeffler, in her book *Let This Be the Time*, gives us some valuable meditation questions to ponder:

> Where do we choose to focus during these years: on our bodies' limitations and aches, on our culture's stereotypes of aging, on life's losses, on our fears and worries? Or do we focus on our blessings with a sense of gratitude, realizing that all is gift: life, people, circumstances, talents, accomplishments, and even struggles?

She quotes Maya Angelou, a wisdom figure for the ages (and the aged), who has said, "If you must look back, do so lovingly. If you must look forward, do so prayerfully. However, the wisest thing you can do is be present in the present...gratefully."

Gratitude is an incredibly important part of a healthy spirituality—never more so than when we are living in the sunset of our lives. A sense of gratitude to God for the many wonderful gifts God has presented to us over the years lays the foundation for a vast array of ways that we can engage with God in prayer. Moreover, when we approach each day with an attitude of gratitude, that predisposition to be thankful acts as a positive influence for the way we live each moment. Living from a place of gratitude can serve as a foundational principle for treating others with respect and working for justice and peace in the world around us and in the world at large.

One of the most widely read and influential mystics of the Church, the fourteenth-century Dominican monk Meister Eckhart, wrote: "Even if the only words you ever say are 'thank you' it would be enough."

At this time of life, as we are perhaps looking to bring a sense of peace and a spirit of goodwill to the core of our being, we must examine our spirituality. A spirituality that embraces the premise that God is our creator, redeemer, and sustainer—the giver of all good gifts, including the gifts of life, love, and all of creation—can serve to buoy us up. The realization that every moment of life is a gift from God, every breath we take is the graceful Spirit of God at work in us, can and will lift the Spirit within us.

Sr. Joan Chittister, writing in *The Gift of Years*, says:

> We have every right to live in gratitude for all the stages of life that brought us here, for the memories that give us great joy, the people who helped us get this far, the accomplishments we carried on our hearts along the way. These experiences cry out to be celebrated. They are no more past than we are. They live in us forever. And I suggest, spending time in prayer with them can bring us a sense of spiritual joy and fulfillment.

FOR REFLECTION: *Begin a "Gratitude List." Write down five things for which you are grateful. Each day add two new items to the list. Continue this practice for days, until you can't think of anything else to add. Review your list frequently.*

FOR READING: *Psalm 100:4–5*

FOR LISTENING: *"All Good Gifts" (John-Michael Tebelak and Stephen Schwartz,* Godspell*); "Table of Plenty" (Dan Schutte)*

5. Dance with the One Who Brought You

Each of us comes into this world though a miraculous process between a man and a woman, including fertilization of an egg, gestation, and birth. The whole process is reliant upon the grace of God, the designer of this awe-inspiring act of creation.

God's gift of life ushered us into this world. God has been with us since the very beginning. Over the course of a busy life, we sometimes lose sight of this fact, or at the very least, it fades into the recesses of our mind. Metaphorically speaking, we forget to "dance with the one who brought us." In other words, we forget the importance of prayer. In retirement, we are given another chance to concentrate on the miracle that we are and to spend time with our creator, savoring that and other miracles, like the miracle of God's unconditional love for us.

In his book *Falling Upward*, Fr. Richard Rohr writes: "Like any true mirror, the gaze of God receives us exactly as we are, without judgment or distortion, subtraction or addition. Such perfect receiving is what transforms us. Being totally received, as we truly are, is what we wait and long for all our lives."

The one who created us is also the one who wants to be *our very best friend*. If this sounds a bit naive or overly simplistic to you, I invite you to spend some time dwelling upon it. Allow our loving God to work with you...in order that you may understand and accept this loving gift more fully.

My friend Rafaela helped me to clearly focus on this important principle. She was a wonderful woman of faith who served on the staff of a parish I visited when I was working for a diocesan office. I was so impressed with her faith, her character, and her love for God that I found my spirit lifted whenever I was with her. One day, during a conversation about her faith, she told me:

I do a lot of driving. Living out here in the country, I am not particularly close to anything except the church, which I can see from my kitchen window. Sometimes, when I am cruising down the highway by myself, I will gently place my hand on the passenger seat next to me. I imagine Jesus sitting there and we talk—about all sorts of things—whatever happens to be on my mind or heart on that particular day.

Rafaela held fast to the realization that Jesus was with her everywhere, all the time, loving her like no one else could. He made his presence known to her via the people with whom she communicated and the situations she encountered each day. For almost eighty years, they "danced" together beautifully! And while I was not with her when she passed into eternal life, I am quite sure that she saved the last dance for her best friend—her loving Lord.

FOR REFLECTION: *Consider the idea that God wants to be your very best friend. Can you embrace that concept? How does it feel? Do you want to pursue it? Why? Why not?*

FOR READING: *Psalm 100 (complete)*

FOR LISTENING: *"Center of My Life" (Paul Inwood); "Praise You with the Dance" (Casting Crowns); "Lord of the Dance" (Sydney Carter)*

6. Mining the Riches of Scripture

Yet just as from the heavens the rain and snow come down and do not return there till they have watered the earth, making it fertile and fruitful, giving seed to the one who sows and bread to the one who eats, so shall my word be that goes forth from my mouth; It shall not return to me empty, but shall do what pleases me, achieving the end for which I sent it. • ISAIAH 55:10–11

A dear friend and spiritual companion suggested that I could not write this chapter without including the above quote from Isaiah. Perhaps no other verses from the Bible capture, more profoundly and poetically, God's promise that the power of sacred Scripture can and does change lives.

Some who read these pages have already discovered this power and taken it to heart. All have probably heard the message, but many have never given Scripture a chance to be life-changing. If you are in this category, jump into the word of God and be ready to have your life changed, forever, for the better.

In my graduate school training in religious education, I was taught and given the opportunity to experience the power of sacred Scripture—especially as a tool for reflection and spiritual growth. There isn't space here for me to go into great detail about what I have learned. However, I can introduce one technique that has had a profound impact on my spiritual growth and on the growth of countless others.

Lectio Divina, sometimes abbreviated to "*Lectio*," can be practiced with various nuances. However, the most common form involves four movements:

1. *Lectio* (reading)—Select a passage from Scripture and read it aloud, slowly and reflectively. This might be a passage from the liturgy of the day, the upcoming Sunday liturgy, or a random passage. (A passage of about eight to fifteen verses is ideal.)

2. *Meditatio* (reflection)—After reading, select a word, phrase, or sentence that speaks to you personally. Spend several minutes meditating on it. What might God be saying to you?

3. *Oratio* (response)—Speak to God about whatever is on your mind or in your heart at this point, based on your reflection.

4. *Contemplatio* (rest)—Let go of all those thoughts and simply rest in God's loving embrace. Attempt to clear your mind so you can listen at the deepest level of your being. Trust that the still, small voice that enlightens your mind and heart at this point will work with your open and trusting spirit to guide whatever action, conversion, or transformation is being presented for your consideration.

A beautiful guiding principle for the practice of *Lectio* is as follows: "The word of God is alive and active and will transform each of us if we open ourselves to receive what God wants to give us."[1]

FOR REFLECTION: *If you have never practiced **Lectio Divina**, I invite you to try it today. If you are already accustomed to **Lectio**, consider using this same technique on passages from other spiritual books or on lyrics from your favorite spiritual songs.*

FOR READING: *Isaiah 55:11; Psalm 119:105*

FOR LISTENING: *"Word of God Speak" (Mercy Me); "Speak Lord, I'm Listening" (John B. Miller/Gary Ault)*

---

1 This principle and the model for *Lectio*, which I have adapted here for space, are from "What is Lectio Divina": http://ocarm.org/en/content/lectio/what-lectio-divina.

7. Prayer as Comfort Food

When I refer to some types of prayer as spiritual comfort food, I don't mean they "taste great" but lack substance or spiritual "nutrition." Rather, as we become more aware of God's promise to love us—and all of creation—unconditionally, we develop a deeper relationship with God. This enriches our prayer life and empowers us to realize, enjoy, and love God more completely. We begin to see God's presence in places where we never noticed it before. We delight in feeling that presence in ways we never felt it before. Simply put, we derive comfort and joy from the idea that our best friend is always with us. Praying to God takes on new dimensions and deeper meaning.

In our retirement years, we will (hopefully) find that we have more time to devote to the pursuit of this deeper relationship with God. All of this is a bit ironic when we come to realize that, as portrayed in Francis Thompson's poem "The Hound of Heaven," *God* has been pursuing *us* for the entirety of our lives.

We can enhance this process of praying more frequently and more deeply when we choose to tie portions of our prayer life into things we naturally like to do.

Stephanie, a retired teacher, is a hiker and a birdwatcher. She loves to walk the trails of the parks in her town, enjoying the landscapes, the foliage, the birds, and other creatures she encounters along the way.

Rita, a successful mathematician and a music lover, marvels at the beautiful sound of a symphony and is also able to appreciate the mathematical intricacies found in the relationships between the various notes in the composition.

Karl is a semi-retired architect. He is fascinated by what humans can accomplish with various kinds of tools, materials, and engineering principles. Like many other spiritual people, he is astounded at the ways that we humans cooperate with God to become co-creators of many marvelous principles and objects we have invented or adapted over the centuries.

Marlene, a medical doctor who no longer has her own practice, volunteers at an urban clinic for under-served populations. She has always been fascinated with the structure and the function of the human body and is astounded by the new medical procedures and treatments that are continuously being discovered.

The list goes on and on. God's handiwork is all around us. *And God's handiwork includes us.*

At this time of life, we have opportunities to slow down and reflect upon the many-splendored aspects of the divine. Such times of quiet and solitude can become invitations to deepen our relationship with our Lord, who is always inviting us into the open arms of an embrace. God's presence is an integral part of each of our lives. When we truly recognize this miracle, life becomes a prayer. How exciting, yet comfortable, that sounds!

FOR REFLECTION: *Think back to an instance when your prayer time was particularly joyful, passionate, energetic, or surprising. What do you think contributed to that feeling?*

FOR READING: *Philippians 4:6–8*

FOR LISTENING: *"Psalm 95—Come Worship the Lord" (John Michael Talbot); "You Are Near" (Dan Schutte)*

8. Love Casts Out Fear

Two of the strongest emotions that can motivate us to action are love and fear. When it comes to making important decisions in our lives, one or the other—and sometimes both—of these feelings are involved.

To be sure, both are important. But, as with everything in life, we must find a way to strike a balance between the two. For example, when traveling in our national parks, I know better than to get too close to a bear. However, from a safe distance I am thrilled at the opportunity to see a bear in the wild. Personally, when I am asked to do something I have never done before, I sometimes experience some fear. I ask myself questions, such as: "What are the risks? What are the benefits? Do I feel called to this task?" If I feel the Holy Spirit encouraging me onward, I try not to let fear paralyze me. With the help of God's grace, I act.

When we keep our loving relationship with God in the forefront of our minds and hearts, we are more apt to make good decisions. When we live a life of gratitude, rooted in joy, we are less likely to let fear become the default switch out of which we operate—the emotional place out of which we make important decisions.

A colleague recently shared a story that illustrates this point:

> While on vacation some years ago in the Caribbean, I happened to have lunch with a trapeze artist from Canada who was retiring from Cirque du Soleil. We were both in our early 60s, and the aerial act he performed the previous evening would be his last because of his retirement. After we talked for a while about his history as an Ontario farm boy who was smitten with the circus, joined up, and eventually worked his way into performing for years in a high-wire act, I finally asked him what he was going to do in retirement. He

responded, with a good deal of excitement in his voice, "Ken, I can't wait to go home and read the next chapter in my life!"

Over the years, Ken has never forgotten this chance (or not-so-chance) encounter. It is part of his life story. He brought it to a conversation he had with a senior lawyer and friend at his law practice.

> I was contemplating retirement from the active practice of law and shared with my friend that my passion for the law and my work was waning. My friend listened, and with a good deal of encouragement and understanding, said: "Ken, your passion isn't *waning*, it is merely *shifting*." I left that conversation with a contented sense that this movement was not simply the end of something but a beginning of an adventure in which God was bringing about new life and a new way of answering his call to loving service.

When we move forward in faith and hope, embracing the love God has for us, seeking and finding ways to respond in love, we realize that we are called to live our lives from the perspective of love, not fear. Remember, "love drives out fear" (1 John 4:18).

FOR REFLECTION: *Have you ever taken a chance on beginning a volunteer/service activity because you felt called—by love—to do it? If so, what did you learn in the process? If not, would you ever consider doing so?*

FOR READING: *Matthew 10:26–27; 1 Corinthians 13 (the whole chapter)*

FOR LISTENING: *"Be Not Afraid" (Bob Dufford, SJ); "Love Like This" (Lauren Daigle)*

9. Discernment—Action—Contemplation, Repeat

Should I seek another companion since my spouse has died? Do I really want that knee replacement I have been thinking about? How do I help my adult daughter who is raising two children on her own? These are difficult decisions. How do we decide what to do in each instance?

When working with my directees about these and other complex situations, I often recommend the process of spiritual discernment, which is an important tool given to us by Saint Ignatius. In his model for spiritual direction, "Discernment is the art of discovering how best to respond to God in daily life." For centuries, people have used Ignatius' rules for discernment to help make wise choices and sound decisions.

> The first principle is a desire to choose the good. As Saint Ignatius put it: "our one choice should be this: I want and I choose what better leads to God's deepening life in me." Saint Ignatius' other rules for discernment help us make choices from among attractive alternatives. Of particular importance are the inner movements of our hearts.[2]

I recently had a session with a directee who is approaching retirement age. An adult male in his mid-60s, his discernment is complicated by a number of circumstances. His employer wants him to delay his retirement because he will be difficult to replace. He has some significant health issues. Although they are not life-threatening, they require a great deal of his time and attention. He has been feeling considerable fatigue, but he is not financially prepared

---

2 Material quoted here is from https//www.loyolapress.com/catholic-resources/ ignatian-spirituality/discernment. Visit this site for more information on the process of discernment.

for total retirement. We are still very much in the midst of his discernment process; however, he is a man of prayer and has a deep desire to follow the Holy Spirit. I am helping him to name the various issues he must confront—especially the spiritual issues—and to develop an action plan for moving forward. The process of discernment, if done properly, is a powerful journey. I am blessed to accompany him in this way.

At some point, it will be time for him to take action regarding his future, based on the information he gleans from his discernment. Once he has acted and has given himself time to see clearly the results of those actions, he will need to reflect and to examine these results. It will probably be helpful for him to invite others who are close to him in this process to share their feedback on what he has accomplished and how he has done it. Then the process begins again: discernment—action—contemplation.

There is a threefold challenge in advancing through this process: first, knowing what gives him energy or fills him with passion; second, knowing what gifts and talents he possesses; and third, learning how his talents and his passions—all gifts from God—can lead him into new and ever more exciting and fruitful activities.

FOR REFLECTION: *Do you have any major decisions to make at this stage of your life? Do a little research on the Ignatian process of discernment. How might this practice be of use to you?*

FOR READING: *Proverbs 16:2–3; Philippians 1:9–11*

FOR LISTENING: *"If We Are the Body" (Casting Crowns)*

10. Dedicate Again!

Webster's New World College Dictionary (fourth edition) defines "dedicate" as "to set apart for worship of a deity or devote to a sacred purpose." I write with that in mind.

In *Four Steps to Spiritual Freedom*, Fr. Thomas Ryan titles Step Four "Daily rededicate your life to God." He writes not only a rationale for the act of rededication but a process we can use to write our own prayer of rededication. Since reading his book over a decade ago, I have found numerous applications for his suggestions within my own life, with none being more practical or more helpful than Step Four.

Ryan's concept for construction of the prayer—a prayer that should be uniquely tailored *by* and *for* each one of us—is based on the premise that, at the deepest level of our spirit, rededication is a willingness to surrender all to God.

For him, rededicating our lives to God daily means constantly asking how we can best use our time, talent, and treasure to love and serve God. The act of rededication is a loving response to a God who is always inviting us deeper into relationship. It is an opportunity to fall in love with God anew each day.

Most days, I recite my own prayer of rededication to our Lord. This is one of the most important things I do on any given day. This simple prayer, which I have constructed in my own words, sets the tone for the day by reminding me that I am dedicating my day, as well as my very being, to the one who gave me life—the one who loves me eternally, immeasurably, and unconditionally. After many years of saying my rededication prayer faithfully, it comes automatically to mind each day.

An example from my working days may illustrate the importance of this principle: As a department director, I sometimes found myself dealing with controversial issues. One day, while waiting for a return phone call from someone who was upset about an important policy that we were implementing, I took a moment to reflect upon my prayer of rededication. When the call came, I calmly and quietly reminded myself that my words and actions were dedicated to God and that God was with me. Although the caller and I were never able to come to total agreement, by God's grace we were able to come to a place of understanding and respect. In that situation and others like it, I have learned many valuable lessons about wisdom, integrity, courage, and the faithfulness of God. And, dear Lord, how I have grown! My prayer of rededication has been a powerful tool for facilitating that growth.

In chapter 2, I wrote about the prayer called the Examen. While praying the Examen is a great way to end the day, the prayer of rededication is a great way to begin it. Consider letting those two forms of prayer form the bookends of each day.

FOR REFLECTION: *Try writing your own prayer for dedicating your life to God. Take your time with it, revising it and praying it until you feel you can comfortably call it your own.*

FOR READING: *Romans 10:9–11; Psalm 86:11–13*

FOR LISTENING: *"Make My Life an Altar" (Cheri Keaggy); "Broken Things" (Matthew West); "Psalm 25—To You, O Lord" (Marty Haugen)*

Being Open
to change

11. Truth and Consequences

One of the most important principles that leads to a sense of peace in our mature years is the habit of being honest—especially when it would be easier to be dishonest.

Sarah, now in her mid-70s, learned the value of truth at an early age. She recalls:

> When I was growing up, my father instilled in us the need to always tell the truth. In some ways, it became our family mantra. And so, as I grew older, being honest became a part of who I am. I internalized honesty and tried very hard to speak the truth in my various professions as well as in my personal life...Sometimes it got me into sticky situations because the other person(s) did not want to hear the truth. In retirement, I have the opportunity to look beyond the truth of mere words and delve into the depth of myself. Who is the true me? What is really important to me? What do I stand for? Do I have any regrets about the choices I've made, or can I accept and live with those consequences? I can see that who I am now is all right. I no longer have to impress anyone; I just have to be comfortable with myself and my God! I stand before God, who is TRUTH in my own truth.

Since I have lived thus far telling the truth, I can now embrace that truth...and the Truth shall set me free!

Sometimes our choice is not between telling the truth or telling a lie but between telling the truth or saying nothing at all. Carl tells of being promoted into an upper-management position in his company. He became one of a dozen vice-presidents, answering only to the president/CEO, named Paul.

One of Paul's stipulations for his VPs was that they never do anything that would embarrass him in front of others. One day, the shoe was on the other foot. A mid-level staffer under Carl's supervision did something that upset Paul. At his next meeting with the VPs, Paul lashed out at Carl for not having more control over those he managed. Carl was upset. Not only did he feel that the CEO's appraisal of the situation was incorrect but, by airing dirty laundry in front of the whole group, Paul was violating his own principle.

Carl knew he had to confront Paul about his inappropriate behavior. It would require speaking truth to power—and Paul was known as a tough taskmaster. At the next meeting between the two, Carl raised the issue. It was a difficult conversation. Never before had Carl had the courage to confront the boss in this way. However, he left the meeting with a feeling of hard-won satisfaction for having spoken his truth to an intimidating boss.

One of the most important goals in life is becoming the most authentic, honest people we can be. Sarah and Carl have worked at that, learning the value of truthfulness and the consequences that come with telling the truth and with not telling the truth.

FOR REFLECTION: *Try to recall a time when telling the truth was particularly difficult for you. How did you handle the situation? Would you do anything differently now? Why or why not?*

FOR READING: *John 8:31–32*

12. Miracle Grow

In his classic book *Falling Upward*, Richard Rohr writes:

> As the body cannot live without food, so the soul cannot
> live without meaning. Victor Frankl described this so well
> when he pointed out that some level of meaning was the only
> thing that kept people in the Nazi concentration camps from
> total despair and suicide during the Holocaust. Humans are
> creators of meaning, and finding deep meaning in our expe-
> riences is not just another name for spirituality but is also the
> very shape of human happiness.

In *The Gift of Years*, Joan Chittister quotes Austrian novelist Marie
von Ebner-Eschenbach, who wrote: "Old age transfigures or fossiliz-
es." This is to say that if we can continue to find meaning in our lives,
we can continue to do great things in our retirement years. If we no
longer believe our lives have purpose, we will not feel fulfilled…and
we will not be happy.

A good friend shared the following story about his father:

> When my father retired, he said he was going to spend the
> first month napping on the couch, and he did just that. My
> mother was afraid that he was going to spend his whole retire-
> ment on the couch. However, after a month or so he was true
> to his vocation as a deacon in the Catholic Church and spent
> the next decade serving the community in many different
> ways. After an appropriate amount of rest and recuperation,

he was able to move forward and to grow as he served others and the Lord.

For some, the retirement years allow us to use talents that we honed during our active careers; for others, those same years afford us the opportunity to explore new and creative avenues that help us find fresh ways to be disciples of Christ.

I was fortunate to be able to leave my full-time job at the age of 63. For years, I had wanted to complete a training program to become a spiritual director. I decided to go for it! As part of the process, I had to do a lot of reading and writing. As I practiced these skills, some old and some new, I realized—with a little help from my friends—that I was being called to write professionally. I have written articles, reflections, and even a couple of books in the past decade, and I enjoy the process immensely. My enthusiasm for life and my desire to help others has grown as a result of these experiences.

Of course, there are often roadblocks to our progress or growth in retirement. Physical, mental, and emotional disabilities can limit what we are able to accomplish. Demands on our available time can come in the form of needing to care for others or for ourselves. The road through retirement is not always smooth, and it's never care-free. But if we keep our eye on the prize—in this case, a purposeful retirement—we can count on the Lord to help us achieve our goals and continue to grow.

FOR REFLECTION: *Staying as active as possible in retirement is a necessary challenge. Are you currently doing things that help you fulfill your sense of purpose as a retired or nearly retired person?*

FOR READING: *Jeremiah 1:4–5*

FOR LISTENING: *"Holy Spirit" (Francesca Battistelli)*

13. The Humble of Heart

"You have been told, O mortal, what is good, and what the Lord requires of you: Only to do justice and to love goodness, and to walk humbly with your God" (Micah 6:8). This is one of my favorite sentences in all of sacred Scripture. There is tremendous power in this beautifully simple statement.

Let's focus for a moment on the final phrase: "to walk humbly with your God." To be humble is to recognize that everyone is a child of God. Everyone is important, loved, and deserving of love. One of the many definitions for the word "humble" resonates well with my perception of the word when used as a spiritual concept. It means to be "of modest pretensions or dimensions." To be humble is to be "grounded." In fact, this word finds its origins in the word *humus*, that is, "of the earth."

To be humble is to know my place in the world—to know that God is God and I am not. Yet, even though I am not God, I am part of something wonderful, something grand. I am a child of God. As such, I am created to love kindness and to do justice.

In chapter 25, I write about my favorite bishop, Maurice Dingman, a former bishop of the Diocese of Des Moines, Iowa. Perhaps what endeared Bishop Dingman to me most was his gentle, genuine humility. When I arrived in Des Moines in 1981 to interview for my first full-time diocesan religious education position, Bishop Dingman knew I was coming. As I entered the parking lot, he was leaving. He stopped, got out of his car, and welcomed me to the diocese. Everyone was important to him! When my father came to visit from Ohio, Bishop Dingman invited Dad, my family, and me to have breakfast with him at his residence. He felt that everyone was to be respected and loved. And the greatest symbol of that love was an invitation to break bread together.

Robert Wicks, in *After Fifty*, lists three essential elements for a well-formed spirituality: love, detachment, and humility. A prerequisite for fully exercising any of those virtues is a genuine knowledge of oneself. He writes: "Both self-knowledge and loving freely and without condition require an openness and a willingness to be vulnerable in a way that can only take hold and grow in an atmosphere of true humility."

Richard Rohr, in his book *Falling Upward*, poetically describes the nature of true humility. "When we can become little enough, naked enough, and honest enough, then we will ironically find that we are more than enough."

Humility is integrally entwined with the concept of surrender to the divine. We can grow to the point where we will surrender our circumstances—our very lives—to God only when we have the self-understanding and humility to appreciate our role in this, God's world!

It is indeed a wonderful irony that we are, each one of us, so tiny yet so significant in the eyes of the Lord.

Humility: it's all about proper perspective.

FOR REFLECTION: *Think of someone you know who is truly humble. What made you think of that person? What would you need to do to become more like them?*

FOR READING: *Philippians 2:3–6; Micah 6:8*

FOR LISTENING: *"This Alone" (Tim Manion); " Shepherd Me, O God" (Marty Haugen)*

14. Say Goodbye—Say Hello!

At this stage of our lives, we have had many opportunities to grieve. Perhaps we have had to say goodbye to parents, siblings, even spouses and other loved ones. Perhaps we have changed careers or relocated for new job opportunities over the years. Perhaps we have broken relationships in our lives that have caused us pain and suffering, like a divorce or an argument with a friend who is now estranged. These are just a few of the many situations we may have faced in our lives that call for us to practice some healthy grieving and move forward. Moreover, retirement itself usually brings forth the need to grieve. The patterns of our days change, and the way we are called to spend our time is altered. Routines that brought a sense of familiarity and comfort are no longer present in our lives; coworkers who became good friends are no longer part of our daily activities.

In our retirement years, we are challenged to transition to new ways of behavior, new routines, and new priorities for our lives. This can also mean that hobbies we have long enjoyed can take on a new significance for us—more time spent with children or grandchildren, more time for gardening, reading, hiking, pickleball, or prayer...and the list goes on.

When I asked a number of my friends (senior citizens like me) to name important things about the retirement years, I was surprised at how many of them focused on the need to make a healthy transition toward retirement.

Helen remarked that it is important to "take time to celebrate and honor the service you have provided over the years" in terms of your career: jobs held and service opportunities in which you have participated. "Celebrate with family as well as the people you have served with over the years. As part of the celebration, be thankful, especially in your spiritual life."

She went on to say: "Have some events, travel, or projects planned for the first several months of retirement to help transition into a new way of living. Think about long-term dreams or ideas of what you want to do in retirement and act upon them."

But, Willard added, "Don't act on them right away!" One of the most important aspects of a healthy transition is taking time to rest. "Don't make any significant commitments to service, volunteer work, or even a part-time job for at least six months." It is very important to give yourself time to rest and to heal from the stress (physical, mental, and/or emotional) that you dealt with in your career. True rest and relaxation are among the greatest sources of healing.

Some of the things that contribute to any grief you might experience may be things you can no longer change (if you ever could). Recognize these, give them to God in prayer, and move on. Other items, such as relationships that might still be reconciled, should be discussed with a trusted friend, a counselor, or a spiritual director, any of whom might help you move forward with a plan for growth and perhaps reconciliation.

Retirement is a big deal...and it's complicated! Give it time, patience, and prayer—not just as you begin but throughout the retirement years. You'll be glad you did!

FOR REFLECTION: *How have you dealt with grief in the past? At this stage of your life, what are you grieving? Grieving is important. How will you proceed to grieve in a healthy way?*

FOR READING: *Romans 8:28; Matthew 11:28–29*

FOR LISTENING: *"Better than a Hallelujah" (Amy Grant); "Blessings" (Laura Story)*

15. Embrace Joy

A joyful heart is an essential quality for a spiritually fulfilling retirement. In Proverbs 17:22, we read: "A joyful heart is the health of the body, but a depressed spirit dries up the bones." The good news is: if you are not living a joyful life, it's not too late to keep some moisture in those bones!

When we begin to see God as the one who will never abandon us, who is our biggest fan, the only one who can and does love us without conditions or restrictions, we are set to begin the experience of a lifetime, the experience of feeling pure joy.

In his book *Chasing Joy*, Fr. Edward Hays presents convincing evidence for the connection between joy and Christian spirituality. He proposes that when the presence of God saturates the totality of our being, this should bring about "ecstatic joy" and "unflappable conviction." God's desire to be infused into every cell of our bodies should "skyrocket us into bliss."

Of course, living a life of joy does not mean we will always feel happy or our lives will be free from suffering and tribulation. It simply means that living in the embrace of God, who loves us unconditionally and who is always with us, can give us the reassurance we need to sustain a measure of hope and joyfulness, no matter the circumstances we face.

When our daughter, Laura, was in high school, she participated in a two-week mission trip to the Dominican Republic. When she returned, I asked her to name her most profound learning from the trip. Almost without hesitation she exclaimed: "I was amazed at how joyful the people were! While they were poor, when measured by the standards of the material world, they had strong, faith-filled families. They looked out for one another. They were very happy, and they welcomed us with open arms."

The members of those families, young and old alike, were demonstrating a principle that Pope Francis (a savvy senior citizen) likes to emphasize. Francis feels that if we truly love Christ and have a sense of how much he must love us, our hearts will "lighten up" with joy, and that joy will radiate to others. Such joy is timeless and knows no boundaries of age or era!

In the inspiring movie *Chariots of Fire*, the protagonist, a remarkable Scottish runner and Olympic medalist named Eric Liddell, is asked why he loves to run. His reply is both spiritual and profoundly joyful: "When I run, I feel [God's] pleasure!" His words are a beautiful testimony to the loving relationship that Liddell had with God and the tremendous joy he felt when he used his talent to give glory to the Lord.

I believe that kind of joy-filled love is what Saint Paul is describing in his letter to the Romans (8:38–39)—the kind of loving relationship God wants for all of us. To fully participate in it, we must first believe in it.

FOR REFLECTION: *Have you ever met someone who radiates the joy of the Lord? What do you feel when you are in the presence of that person? If you desired to become more like them, what do you think you would need to do?*

FOR READING: *John 16:22; Romans 8:38–39*

FOR LISTENING: *"Good to Be Alive" (Jason Gray); " Companions on the Journey" (Carey Landry)*

16. Play...Then Play Some More!

I've always had a bit of a wit and a sense of playfulness. At times, this has convinced some people to label me as "silly" or "goofy" and to wonder if I will ever "act my age." In my early adulthood, I sometimes felt self-conscious about it. But, over time, I realized that it was a gift and that I should be grateful for my lighthearted attitude. On more than one occasion I have used my sense of humor and playfulness to lighten the mood of someone else or to bring myself out of an emotional slump.

Over the years, my wife and I have learned to be more playful with each other, and it has served us well. We have grown closer, using the gifts of humor and joy to bolster each other emotionally—and spiritually. And we've managed, by the grace of God, to pass this playfulness on to our daughter. Or perhaps I should say she has helped us to develop and practice it more fully, adding her own exuberance and joy to the mix.

I will never forget the day Laura (our daughter) came home from choir practice and told us of a conversation she'd had with the choir director at church, Mrs. Ross. Laura was regaling Mrs. Ross with a story about some hilarious antics the three of us were engaged in at home. When she finished talking, Mrs. Ross said, "You folks must laugh all the time at your house." Laura paused for a moment and then replied, "Yes, I guess we do laugh a lot." At that moment I realized how blessed we are as a family to enjoy that gift together.

Of course, life can be difficult at times. It's not all fun and games. There are times when playfulness is not the appropriate response. However, there are also times when a sense of playfulness can cut through a difficult situation and bring some relief...even healing.

Sometimes, in these senior years, playfulness comes easily. Perhaps we have grandchildren who are an absolute joy to play with, joke with, and party with on birthdays, holidays, and other special occasions. However, we do not all have such opportunities. In that case, it is even more important to find something to do that will make us laugh. It may be sharing funny remembrances with friends, enjoying word games or cards, going to a ball game, watching a favorite comedy, or revisiting the music that made us smile and dance decades ago. Find ways to play—and do them. Ideally, you can do them with other people. When necessary, do them alone.

God wants us to be happy and rejoices when we rejoice. If you have the gift of playfulness in your toolbox, rejoice in it and cultivate it. If you don't have that gift, try to surround yourself with others who have it. Let them teach you how to play. It is good for the spirit—good for the soul.

FOR REFLECTION: *Whom do you know that you would consider playful? What do you think makes them that way? Consider asking them that question.*

FOR READING: *Proverbs: 17:22; 2 Samuel 6:5*

FOR LISTENING: *"Companions on the Journey" (Carey Landry); "Canticle of the Turning" (Rory Cooney)*

17. Make Yourself a Pretzel

To live is to change, and to be perfect is to have changed often. • **SAINT JOHN HENRY CARDINAL NEWMAN**

Only God is perfect, but this quotation from Cardinal Newman does reinforce the principle that change and the flexibility it requires are important aspects of a life well lived.

The ability to change is a sign of growth. Of course, some change comes naturally to us. As we age, every part of us changes. The better we are at adapting to changes in our lives, the more we will be able to feel at home in our bodies, minds, and spirits.

Change is often a sign of personal growth, aided by prayer and deep reflection. It is the ability to remain flexible in the face of new information and to be courageous in changing paths or forging a new path altogether when necessary.

The art of change, if we may call it that, can be guided by a process often referred to as discernment. In the spiritual tradition of Saint Ignatius of Loyola, discernment is defined as "the art of discovering how best to respond to God in daily life," as Loyola Press has put it.[3]

One key to a good discernment process is courage: not allowing irrational fear or anxiety to stand in the way of your decision-making process.

Harry tells the story of attending a presentation by a Christian theater company many years ago at a chapel on a military base where he was stationed. He was so moved by their ministry that he contemplated signing up to become part of the missionary theater group when his four-year stint in the military was complete. However, the notion seemed a bit far-fetched—even to him—at first.

A more traditional career path seemed more sensible. But the more he discerned, the more convinced he became: this was what he was being called to do.

He remembers well the evening he sat down with his parents to inform them of the results of his discernment process. Harry expected that his father, a practical businessman, would be quick to decry the foolishness of spending time in this theater group when, at the age of 25, he should be establishing himself in a career. To Harry's surprise and delight, his father said: "You seem to be very interested in this. If you are ever going to do something of this nature, this is the time. You are single, with no commitments to a wife, children, or an employer."

That was forty-seven years ago. Harry pursued this path and met a lovely member of the company who would eventually become his

---

3 The principles for spiritual discernment as outlined by Saint Ignatius can be found on the Press's website: https://www.loyolapress.com.

wife. They have both had creative and fulfilling lives in Christian education ministries. They are retired now and very grateful for the courage they found along the way—the courage to be open to the Lord's call and the commitment to see it through...a commitment that often required prayerful discernment and the flexibility to make adjustments to their plans when necessary. In their senior years, the ability to be flexible is perhaps more important than ever.

FOR REFLECTION: *Can you think of a time in your life when you had to be particularly flexible? How well did you respond to that challenge?*

FOR READING: *John 4:4–30*

FOR LISTENING: *"All that Is Hidden" (Bernadette Farrell)*

18. Only God Is Perfect

We can be our own harshest critics. This is evidenced by the fact that, at some point, almost every individual who enters into spiritual direction with me says something that indicates they are locked in a cycle of guilt and shame that keeps them from fully opening to the love and mercy God has for them.

In her excellent book *Let This Be the Time*, Janet Schaeffler writes:

> I must learn to forgive myself for all the mistakes I've made in my life. I need to recognize that no one is perfect, so I shouldn't expect perfection from myself. Rather, I need to focus on these mistakes as an opportunity to grow in love of God and all creation.... One of the functions of our eldering

years is to become comfortable with who we are rather than to lament what we are not.

As we move into our retirement phase, we may confront a bitter irony. Over the years, we can become more set in our ways, finding it harder and harder to lighten up on ourselves. This can happen at the time of life when we want to come to terms with who we are and find peace in our relationships with others and within ourselves.

Sometimes, this circumstance is complicated by factors such as perfectionism (a possible indicator of obsessive-compulsive disorder, or OCD) or simply by years of practicing unhealthy behaviors. The seeds of these negative thoughts and behaviors can come from either nature (genetic disposition) or nurture (the way we are raised)—or, most likely, they are the result of a combination of those factors. In any case, the behaviors and the thoughts that drive them can be very difficult to change. But the work to change them is worth it.

I know this because I was such a person as a child and young adult. Only with a good support group, including loving parents and friends, counselors and spiritual directors—as well as medication for anxiety—have I learned to embrace my goodness and accept my flaws while striving each day to grow closer to God, who loves me without reservation.

When I recognize a tendency in one of my directees toward what seems like OCD, I recommend they seek counseling and talk to their doctor as well as continuing to allow me to help them with the spiritual aspects of their compulsive thoughts.

For those who do not have perfectionistic tendencies, I recommend time spent contemplating God's incredible unconditional love for us and how that love is manifested through other people, the beauty of nature, the wonders of the arts, and especially through prayer and spiritual reading. We can concentrate on the many ways that God reaches out to us in the course of any given day. Moreover,

I remind them of the wisdom of those who have come before us in faith. Take, for example, Native Americans who have woven the "God's Eye." It always includes a tiny mistake or imperfection to remind each of us that we are not God. And since we are not God, we should not expect to be perfect. What a relief!

FOR REFLECTION: *Is there something in the way you see yourself that makes it difficult to love yourself or to accept the beautiful love God has for you? If so, do you have the courage to talk with someone you trust about your feelings?*

FOR READING: *2 Corinthians 12:9*

FOR LISTENING: *"Don't Try So Hard" (Amy Grant with James Taylor); "Truth Be Told" (Matthew West); "Grace Wins" (Matthew West)*

19. Detachment

The *Oxford World Dictionary* defines detachment as "The state of being objective." The Alcoholics Anonymous movement uses the term "emotional detachment" to describe the process of disconnecting from the emotional pull that an addict can have over family and friends. In either case, such objectivity is generally considered a gift to be cultivated.

In the spiritual sense, detachment deals with recognizing those things that keep us from fully loving and worshiping God. Indeed, a healthy objectivity when dealing with life's circumstances frees us so we can more easily listen to the voice of the Holy Spirit. To successfully practice the art of objectivity/detachment, we must possess comprehensive self-knowledge. That is to say, we must understand who we are, how we function, and what we value in life.

In his book *After 50: Spiritually Embracing Your Own Wisdom Years*, Robert Wicks offers this explanation of the process: "Without self-knowledge we are...unable to recognize the idols from which we need to detach ourselves in order to meet God. Consequently, in such instances, we cannot develop the detachment necessary for the true caring and compassion of unselfish love."

Detachment can be difficult to achieve. We need help. Wicks continues:

> Whether it is a problematic relationship, a bad habit or an addiction...the important goal for all of us is to share our inability to let go of something with God, instead of hiding it. Hiding things from God goes hand in hand with hiding things from ourselves. Recognizing problems even in prayer, maybe especially in prayer, is a good initial step in addressing them in life.

Often, a key to detachment is the ability to put our lives into context. Valerie Schultz, in an article titled "The Secret to Aging—Physically and Spiritually—with Grace," published in *America* magazine (August 4, 2022, online edition) frames it this way:

> Maybe the secret to aging gracefully is underscoring that we have already made a lifetime of progress on our spiritual work. We can't stop time, but we can befriend it, be kind to it, rather than race against it. We can put one old trudging foot in front of the other. We may have to slow our pace a bit on our walk to God's finish line. We're going to get there all the same.

When dealing with a difficult person or circumstance, I imagine we have all been told by a friend or confidant that we are too close to the situation. We must step back in order to get a better perspective. This nugget of wisdom is beckoning us to try to be more objective by taking our biases out of the equation, putting ourselves in another person's shoes, thinking about the bigger picture. Any or all of these approaches can help us prepare to hear the voice of God speaking to us in the silence of our hearts.

FOR REFLECTION: *My friend Bishop Dingman used to say that everybody worships something or someone. Some worship God; others worship money or power or fame. Is there anything you worship more than you worship God—anything you put ahead of God in your life? (Try to be honest!) Only when we can recognize a flaw in our belief system can we possibly change it.*

FOR READING: *Romans 8:5*

FOR LISTENING: *"These Alone Are Enough" (Dan Schutte); "I Shall Not Want" (Audrey Assad)*

20. Creativity

I have loved music for as long as I can remember. I was born into a golden age of music. From the late 1950s through the '60s and '70s, classic rock-and-roll was king. Ever since I was in middle school, I've wanted to sing in a rock band. I don't have a great voice, but it's a good voice. I have sung in choirs and cantored at church over the years.

As a child, I loved listening to the stories of my parents, grandparents, aunts, and uncles. They would often sit around our picnic table in summertime and regale each other (and us) with tales from their youth, at once both touching and funny.

In my late 20s, I entered graduate school. Much to my surprise, I discovered that I enjoyed writing research papers. The creative energy I derived from the process of learning history, facts, and ways of thinking, then collecting the concepts and getting them all down on paper, energized me.

Singing, listening, and writing: these talents served me well in my career as a Christian educator, but they were not at the center of my life. I often found myself wishing I could do more with these gifts I had received. I wanted to create. But the obligations of daily life—family, career, etc.—kept me from pursuing any of these passions with energy or consistency.

In midlife I discovered a wonderful book by Fr. Thomas Ryan titled *Soul Fire: Accessing Your Creativity*. Ryan insists that "Creativity is something we all have, and there are myriad possibilities for the expression of our creative energies...Carl Jung, one of the founders of modern psychology, believed that the second half of life was the crucial time to recognize, take ownership of, and express our creative energies." Research has indicated that honoring and expressing creativity during our senior years often leads to new and deepening friendships. It lifts morale by giving us a sense of accomplishment and can even help us shape the legacy we hope to leave for those who follow us.

It is never too late to realize and develop your creativity by focusing on the things that give you energy and joy. As a good listener, with training in theology and spirituality, I have become a spiritual director. As a person who enjoys writing, I have been a contributing writer to magazines and books. However, there is one unquenched fire that still burns within me. I have never joined a rock-and-roll band. I do have a friend who has a band, though. Hmmm...There's food for thought!

I had the distinct pleasure of meeting Fr. Ryan a few years ago. I asked him to sign my copy of *Soul Fire*. His written message that accompanied the signature conveyed his wish for me concerning my own creative energy. "To Bill, Blow on the coals 'til they rise up and dance!" May it be so for you as well!

FOR REFLECTION: *Try this brainstorming exercise: Think of activities you could participate in that would feed your passion for life—for living. Be bold! Be creative! Next, prioritize that list. What would enflame your passion most fervently? Then, imagine what you might do to "blow on the coals" of your soul.*

FOR READING: *John 15:5*

FOR LISTENING: *"Canticle of the Sun" (Marty Haugen); "Sing Out, Earth and Skies" (Marty Haugen)*

CONCENTRATING ON RELATIONSHIP BUILDING

21. Holy Listening

I love talking about listening. Funny—as I write that sentence, it sounds like an oxymoron. If I am talking about listening, I must not be listening! Perhaps I should say: There is a time for listening and a time for speaking. That puts things in perspective.

Let's explore several types of "holy listening." Marci, who has lived alone for the past thirty years—ten of those in retirement—speaks about her holy listening: "Retirement brings added meaning to QUIET…SOLITUDE. [It] 'tunes me in' to the furnace going on… to the call of the mourning dove…to the sounds of quiet. I have acquired a knack for praising God in that stillness, and that knack becomes a part of who I am as I practice it." Marci and many others find that the Holy Spirit speaks to their hearts during this special time of prayer.

Barbara, a grandmother who retired from a career in education, is still learning the art of holy listening.

> My husband and I were babysitting our darling grandkids recently at their home. I decided I wanted to teach our four-year-old granddaughter to garden—well, really to pull the many weeds in their flower garden. So, I brought my gardening bag and tools and a pair of gardening gloves for her. She was absolutely delighted to learn just how to be a gardener.

I told her to get all the weeds out. "Well," she said to me in reply, "G'ma, we don't have to get all the weeds out, we just have to try our best and believe in ourselves." A bit of profound wisdom from a four-year-old. I find if I just listen, she has so much to teach me.

It seems that holy listening is becoming a lost art in our society. Many of us move at a frantic pace that puts a premium on getting things done. All too often, stopping to thoughtfully listen to another human being is an unwanted distraction. Also, the venom frequently heard in such circumstances as the political discourse of the day does not entice one person to really listen to another. Therein lies the ultimate definition of holy listening: not that we must agree with every speaker but that we must honor their right to speak. For they, too, are a child of God, just as we are!

And there is the age-old problem of the listener who is not really concentrating on the speaker; instead, they are thinking about how they will respond to what they think the speaker is saying.

In the more intimate moments of dialogue, in those special moments when a family member or friend comes to us with a situation they need to talk through, make a concerted effort to settle yourself and concentrate on what they are saying. If possible, watch for nonverbal cues such as facial expressions and body movement. Try to be as objective as possible. Help them relax. Don't worry about trying to respond with the perfect answer to their conundrum. If a suggested action comes to mind, feel free to share it. But remember, often the person is just looking for a good listener—a holy listener—to accompany them as they sort things out for themselves.

FOR REFLECTION: *Recall a time when you, as a listener, did not practice what you would consider "good listening skills." How might you practice this "holy listening" in a similar conversation the next time?*

FOR READING: *Hebrews 13:1–2; 1 Samuel 3:9–10*

FOR LISTENING: *"The Irish Blessing" (The Irish Blessing 2020); "There Is a Longing" (Anne Quigley); "I Will Lift My Eyes" (Bebo Norman)*

22. Giving *Is* Receiving

"I don't know what your destiny will be, but one thing I know, the only ones among you who will really be happy are those who have sought and found how to serve."

• **ALBERT SCHWEITZER**

These words are a wonderful invitation for each of us to contemplate the importance of offering our gifts and talents in service to those in need. In fact, many respected leaders have offered similar thoughts to ponder. In his inaugural speech, President John F. Kennedy said: "Ask not what your country can do for you, ask what you can do for your country." Jewish theologian Martin Buber eloquently stated: "He who loves brings God and the world together." And Robert K. Greenleaf, well-known author of the groundbreaking book *Servant Leadership*, penned these words: "Servant leaders are healers in the sense of making whole by helping others to a larger and nobler vision and purpose than they would likely attain for themselves." Simply yet profoundly, Mother Teresa said: "A life not lived for others is not a life." And many of us have seen pictures of Pope Francis washing the feet of the incarcerated.

Most, if not all, of the aforementioned leaders took a cue from a true servant-leader, Jesus Christ. While we may not think of ourselves as leaders in the mold of Jesus, Mother Teresa, or Schweitzer, the fact is we are leaders just by the way we act. Leading by example is perhaps the most powerful type of leadership—and all of us are given the opportunity to participate in that.

Some of my retired friends commented on the importance of service. Mary said she thinks about ways she can deepen her spiritual life that offer her meaning by giving her opportunities to serve others. Rebecca has tried to focus on one or two ways in which she feels called to serve. For her, this involves offering special care to her husband, who has a terminal illness, as well as spending quality time with her grandchildren.

Anything we do, if we do it with love and care, serves to build the reign of God right here on earth. In that sense, we become co-creators with God. Think about that for a moment. The architects and contractors who design and build a building, the nurse who cares for the sick, the teacher who educates students, the lawyer who champions the rights of others, the janitor who scrubs a floor—all are doing good service in the world.

Today, take a few moments to celebrate the good service you have accomplished in your life. Then, set out to explore how you can use your remaining time, energy, and talent to continue to make the world a better place. Giving added purpose to your life in this way—and offering it to the Lord—can provide you with a deep and abiding sense of comfort and joy. Our loving and creative God has invited us all to be co-creators in service to God's world. How will we respond?

FOR REFLECTION: *Reread the final paragraph of this reflection. Then consider acting on it.*

FOR READING: *Galatians 5:13–14; John 12:26*

FOR LISTENING: *"The Servant Song" (Richard Gillard);
"Do Something" (Matthew West); "They'll Know We Are Christians
by Our Love" (Peter Scholtes)*

23. Storytime, Part 1

Each of us has stories to tell: stories about the people we've met,
places we've been, things we've experienced, and lessons we've
learned. Collectively, these vignettes form the story of our lives. Just
as the characteristics of our minds and bodies are represented by
our DNA, many of the details of our lives and our personalities are
represented in the stories we tell.

Once we acknowledge that a story has the power to shape us, we
must spend time reflecting upon it. We do this by asking ourselves
questions, such as: What actually happened? Who was involved?
Where did it happen? How did I feel as things unfolded? What did
I learn as a result of this incident? These and other such questions
help us process the story—to mine it for the riches it may contain.
As we engage with our stories over time, we become better at recognizing their significance and verbalizing those insights to others who
might benefit from hearing them. In doing so, we knit the fabric of
relationships with other people and ultimately with God. And there
we are again, right back to the importance of building relationships,
the lifeblood of a life well lived. Spending time with our stories is
crucial. Sharing our stories with others and listening to their stories
is vitally important as well.

Fred Rogers, a Presbyterian minister also known as Mister
Rogers of PBS television fame, carried in his wallet a quote from
a social worker he once met. It said: "Frankly, there isn't anyone

you couldn't learn to love once you've learned their story." For many years, he embodied that philosophy on his award-winning show, *Mister Rogers' Neighborhood*. He taught countless children—and adults as well—not to be quick to judge others. Get to know their stories.

Not long ago, I experienced the very essence of what Mister Rogers was constantly teaching on his show. At a retreat, I met a man, Dale, I had known professionally a number of years before. Back then, our similar careers brought us together several times each year. I had never tried to get to know him very well because I was uncomfortable around him. He seemed aloof and at times harsh or unfeeling.

At the retreat, we ended up together in a small group and he shared a story. He talked about how he had found fruitful self-understanding by reflecting on his successes and failures over the years. In the process, he had realized that he was indeed sometimes cold, aloof, harsh, and controlling in his relationships with others, both in his personal life and professionally. He regretted those actions now and had sought to make amends where possible. Of equal importance, he had shared his newfound wisdom with his (now adult) children. He explained:

> I wanted them to know that my unconscious negative behavior may have affected how they see themselves and why they act the way they do. And I wanted them to reflect on that as well, for their own personal health, and in relationships with their spouses, children, and others.... My growing, more honest self-understanding continues to help me improve as a person.

In the next chapter, I will finish this story and say more on the topic of "Storytime."

FOR REFLECTION: *Who are some of your favorite storytellers? What makes their stories special for you?*

FOR READING: *Matthew 13:10–16; Matthew 13:24–43*

FOR LISTENING: *"My Story" (Big Daddy Weave)*

24. Storytime, Part 2

"Every good story is about conversion," retired Auxiliary Bishop Robert F. Morneau of the Diocese of Green Bay, Wisconsin, used to say. Whether the story describes a shift in someone's way of thinking or acting or it causes others to change their ways, a good story always does seem to have something to do with conversion.

The story that Dale recalled for us at the retreat—a story I told in the previous chapter—is a wonderful example of this. Dale came to a realization that caused him to alter the course of his life. The story of how he put that decision into action is very moving, especially for those of us who have known him for many years and are now experiencing the fruits of his conversion. Many of our most powerful life lessons are transmitted through stories. In the powerful conversion story of the Academy Award-winning movie *Driving Miss Daisy*, Miss Daisy learns to love and respect the chauffeur who drives her car. At first, he is no more than a hired hand in her eyes, with nothing to offer her beyond his driving skills. Eventually, they form a bond that enriches both their lives. In the process of her change of heart, Daisy gives us a lot to ponder about the spiritual importance of *metanoia*, or conversion.

A powerful story, widely distributed, has the ability to affect the thought processes of countless numbers of people. However, this is not always a good thing. For the story to have a positive effect, it must be rooted in truth. Such things as lying, taking the truth out of context, or manipulating it to serve an evil purpose can do great damage. Dr. David Walsh, an internationally known psychologist and media consultant, cautions us that "Whoever tells the stories defines the culture." He is referring to the stories we hear each day via news coverage, advertisers, talk-show hosts, and the countless others who present the stories we ingest through the various media prevalent in our world today. His statement is an important reminder that the quality and integrity of the story are significant properties. We must sift through the stories carefully in search of the truth.

Scripture is full of stories; each one is meant to help us know more about our salvation history. The stories we read about Jesus in the gospels are particularly important for teaching us how to live as missionary disciples of Christ. In fact, the parables, stories that Jesus used as particular teaching tools, are among the most significant stories of all. Together, the stories in the Bible form the narrative that theologians (and at least one Hollywood producer, George Stevens) have called "the greatest story ever told." Moreover, our Christian tradition is filled with wonderful stories of saints who have done marvelous things, giving glory to God in the process.

The stories of our individual lives summarize who we are. When those stories include connections with and reflections on the stories of our Christian faith, we have the material for a tapestry of living, loving, and being loved in a fashion that gives vibrant detail and meaning to our love affair with our wonderful God.

FOR REFLECTION: *Spend a few moments thinking about a favorite family occasion. How would you tell the story of that event to a friend?*

FOR REFLECTION: *Have you ever changed your way of thinking or acting in response to a story you experienced?*

FOR READING: *John 4:5–42; Mark 4:1–20*

FOR LISTENING: *"Beautiful, Beautiful" (Francesca Battistelli);*
"Testify to Love" (Avalon or Wynonna Judd)

25. Integrity

My good friend Blain told me a story years ago that I have never forgotten.

He was on a retreat with six members of his staff, and they were asked to participate in the following exercise.

They were each given a piece of newsprint and instructed to tape it to the wall. Then they were given markers and told to start with their own paper and write as many positive personality traits (gifts) as they could write about themselves. After that, they were to proceed in turn to each of the remaining six papers and do the same thing for each person. When all were finished, they took time to discuss what had been written on each paper and why it was written.

For Blain, it was both affirming and enlightening. For example, one staff member wrote the word "integrity" on Blain's newsprint. Blain had a vague notion of what the word meant but decided to look it up in the dictionary to get a clear definition. According to *Webster's New World College Dictionary*, integrity means "The quality or state of being of sound moral principle, uprightness, honesty and sincerity." He thought to himself: "What a terrific trait! It is more than just being honest (important as that is); it is more than being of sound moral principle (a wonderful thing in itself); it is more than being sincere." Blain was honored to receive this compliment. In his mind, it was one of the nicest things one person could ever say to another. Since that day, he has tried to live up to that compliment: to practice integrity in all his relationships.

I have met other people like Blain—people who demonstrated remarkable integrity. The first bishop who employed me as a staff member was Maurice Dingman (now deceased) of Des Moines, Iowa. Bishop Dingman was known for taking courageous stands on significant, often controversial, justice issues. One day, several of us were returning with him from a meeting in a rural part of the diocese. He had recently taken a public stand in favor of family farms that were being squeezed out of existence by larger corporate farms. Some business leaders and politicians were very upset with him. I asked him what it was like for him, being embroiled in a major controversy. He simply said, "Bill, at my age [he was in his mid-60s at the time], I have learned not to worry about what other people think of me or what they might threaten to do to me. I just try to live each day being true to God—and true to myself."

Richard Rohr, in his book *Falling Upward*, wrote that those who possess integrity can "aid and influence other people simply by being who they are. Human integrity probably influences and moves people from potency to action more than anything else." It changes the world for the better. No matter our ages, each of us still has time to work on this excellent virtue, remembering that acting with integrity brings goodness and peace of mind, especially in our senior years, as we strive to put our affairs in order.

FOR REFLECTION: *Name a friend or relative who possesses or possessed the virtue of integrity.*

FOR REFLECTION: *Do you believe you are (for the most part) a person of integrity? Why or why not?*

FOR READING: *Luke 8:11–15*

FOR LISTENING: *"Open My Eyes" (Jesse Manibusan); "Seek Ye First" (Karen Lafferty)*

26. Forgiveness, Part 1

If you were to ask a dozen people to give you a list of the most important characteristics of a healthy spirituality, you would probably get twelve distinct lists. However, one characteristic that would likely appear on each of those lists is forgiveness: both the desire to seek it and the need to grant it. At no time is this more important than it is for those of us in the sunset of our lives.

Because we are human, not divine, we have all experienced both situations where we have offended someone and those where we have been offended. All too often, these events have caused deep hurt, leaving emotional scars. In some cases, the wounds have never completely healed. They continue to fester and, in the process, they keep us from finding the peace that we so desperately long for. And the longing becomes more intense as we grow older. Constructively dealing with and learning from these difficult circumstances is a necessary prerequisite for moving our lives into harmony with the message and mission of Jesus Christ—and finding peace.

Author and retreat leader Sr. Janet Schaeffler tells this story in her book *Let This Be the Time*: "During a recent retreat day, when I asked the people what they thought was the most important task of the eldering years, the vast majority named forgiveness. Carol (a participant) remarked: 'I've told God not to call me yet; I still have lots of forgiving to do and it's taking me lots of time.'"

Indeed, forgiving and asking for forgiveness are hard work. But both actions are profoundly important for our spiritual and emotional growth. Joan Chittister, in her book *The Gift of Years*, writes: "Forgiveness puts life back together again. It is proof of our own learnings. It is sign of our own inner healing...It is the measure of the divine in us."

But still, *it is so difficult!* This realization begs a couple of questions: How can I get to that place where I can find the courage to ask for forgiveness from someone? Where do I find the mercy to grant forgiveness to one who has wounded me? In chapter 3, on trust, surrender, and patience, you will find a clue to these answers. Asking forgiveness and granting forgiveness are made possible by the grace of God working within us. Sr. Janet, in her book quoted above, eloquently writes:

> Forgiveness, above all, is a power from God; it is not something that we can do alone but only with God's strength and grace. When we forgive, we are acting in a Godlike way; we are living the image of God in which we were created. If we need a teacher and a guide in how to do this, it pervades the gospels; Jesus taught us forgiveness in his teachings but also ardently in his life.

In the next chapter, I will share a story that has helped me understand and appreciate the value of forgiveness.

FOR REFLECTION: *Do you have relationships in your life that ache for the balm of forgiveness, either asking for it or granting it? If so, how would you like to proceed with these situations?*

FOR READING: *Luke 15:11–32; Matthew 18:21–22*

FOR LISTENING: *"Forgiveness" (Matthew West); "Come as You Are" (Crowder)*

27. Forgiveness, Part 2

Forgiveness is difficult to put into practice for a number of reasons. For one thing, it goes against our instincts. When we are hurt, we tend to want to fight back, to get even, to settle the score. Moreover, it calls for deep and candid introspection. We must ask ourselves several questions:

- Can I recognize how I have contributed to this rupture in relationship that is causing tension and pain?

- Am I willing to take responsibility for my actions and to apologize for anything I did that contributed to this difficult situation?

- Am I willing to admit that I have things to learn about the fragile but important nature of human relationships?

- Am I willing to act on my learnings, thereby giving evidence of a conversion—a change of heart?

- Even if I am willing to forgive/seek forgiveness, can I accept that the other person may not be willing to do the same?

Only if we are able to answer yes to each of these questions are we prepared to seek and to grant forgiveness. How might such a scenario play out in real life?

Megan was a shift supervisor for nurses on a wing of a local hospital. Over the years, she worked hard to become an advocate for both the patients and the nurses under her care. At one point, over a period of months she felt that her wing was being overlooked for upgrades to equipment and programs designed to make the rigors of nursing more manageable and more pastoral. Funding that she felt should be coming to her seemed to be going to Bridget, the supervisor in another wing. Correctly or incorrectly, Megan felt that the head of nursing favored Bridget. Megan made a derogatory comment to some of her nurses about Bridget. The comment got back to Bridget and she wasted no time retaliating. She started a nasty rumor about Megan, based on what Megan insisted was unsubstantiated innuendo.

Now it was Megan's turn to be offended. Many months went by, and Megan and Bridget were unable to reconcile their differences. Eventually, both women retired from nursing without solving the conflict. Megan was stuck. She had been carrying this mixed bag of sorrow, anger, and guilt, and it was hampering her emotional and spiritual growth.

Megan was committed to finding a way forward in this dilemma. She told her story to her spiritual director, who listened attentively and said, "You might consider how to deal with the parts of this story you have some control over and how to surrender the remaining parts to God." Megan took time to think and pray about what her director had said. At her next appointment, with the help of her director, she wrote a letter to Bridget in which she took responsibility for things she did that contributed to the rift between them. She also prayed for the grace to release the anger in her heart in order to forgive Bridget. Megan then sent the letter. To my knowledge, she never received a reply. Even so, she feels she acted with integrity, applying the principles of forgiveness. For her part, she has forgiven Bridget. The remainder is out of her control; she has placed it in God's hands. What better place could there be for it?

FOR REFLECTION: *Is there anything in this chapter that can be useful to you as you discern how to proceed with the process of forgiving and/or asking for forgiveness?*

FOR READING: *Matthew 18:21–35; Matthew 6:14*

FOR LISTENING: *"Reckless Love" (Corey Asbury); "Let There Be Peace on Earth" (Jill Jackson and Sy Miler); "Heart of God" (Zach Williams)*

28. Mentoring

John has been in positions of leadership many times in his life. Naturally, he has spent considerable time reading articles and books about the practice of leadership. Recently, he told me that he has seen an increase in the number of references to the concept of mentoring.

Many businesses, both for-profit and not-for-profit, have established programs to mentor their workers, pairing a wiser and more experienced worker with a less experienced one. A less formal but equally effective approach to mentoring is being lived out daily in many volunteer organizations and even in families, where grandparents are helping to raise their grandchildren.

Among the greatest opportunities that our senior years can provide is the opportunity to offer our knowledge and experience to others who need the wisdom and skills we have gleaned as a result of our own life journeys.

Richard Rohr, writing in *Falling Upward*, speaks of us as "elders." "Such elders are the 'grand' parents of the world. Children and other adults feel so safe and loved around them, and they themselves feel so needed and helpful to children, teens and mid-life adults. And they are. They are in their natural flow."

From my work in campus ministry and spiritual direction, I would go a step further. I have found that even young adults, ages 18 to 40, are hungry for the wisdom of seniors. This is especially true when they are facing major decisions about such issues as choosing a career and a life partner.

Of course, the role of a mentor is a two-way street, offering potential benefits to both the older and the younger person in the mentoring relationship. This is especially significant with regard to the relationships between senior citizens and children. In *The Gift of Years*, Sr. Joan Chittister writes: "Intergenerational friendships between an older and a younger one are as important to the elder as they are to the child…Children give us a lifeline to the present and the future…Children release the child in us before it completely withers up and goes away."

Unfortunately, some seniors miss the opportunities they are given in which they could be mentors. They simply don't realize or appreciate the role to which they are being called. The philosopher Cicero had a great take on this problem, as Chittister points out in *The Gift of Years*: "The older generation has a great deal to give the world. But first they must come to value it themselves." She also notes that mentoring empowers the mentor to become the best self he or she can be and to help others do the same. In *Let This Be the Time*, Sr. Janet Schaeffler cleverly comments that "Adding an 's' to the beginning of the word 'age' gives us 'sage.'"

Alcoholics Anonymous, one of the most powerful spiritual and psychological programs of the twentieth century, asserts that a person must pass along the benefits of his or her hard-won wisdom or there has been no real gift at all. That is how important the concept of mentoring is.

FOR REFLECTION: *In what way(s) are you uniquely qualified to be a mentor? Who might you mentor?*

FOR READING: *Proverbs 3:13–18*

FOR LISTENING: *"Day by Day" (Stephen Schwartz, **Godspell**); " Let Us Be Bread" (Thomas J. Porter)*

29. Relationships = Life Support

The young apprentice asked the wise man: "Sir, what is the meaning of life?" The wise man replied: "The meaning of life is found in relationships: relationships with God, with others, and with self."

Now that I'm in my mid-70s, I understand the meaning of that answer more than ever. Moreover, I have noticed that these relationships often become intertwined. The way I interact with others can have a profound effect on my relationship with God and with myself. And I know that I still have lessons to learn, relationships that need work, and love to give and to receive. Our relationships should form the heart of who we are, how we live, and what we value.

I invite you to place yourself inside one or more of the stories that follow. What can you learn from them about the significance of meaningful relationships in your life?

> One day, a woman's little girl arrived home late after school. The mother was so angry that she started to yell…However, after about five minutes she suddenly stopped and asked: "Why are you so late, anyway?" The daughter replied: "Because I had to help another girl who was in trouble." [The mother said,] "Well, what did you do to help her?" The daughter replied: "Oh, I sat down next to her and helped her cry."[4]

> One day Tom came into Dan's small local hardware store and bought several hundred dollars in plumbing supplies. Dan spent thirty minutes explaining how the various items could be used to complete the plumbing project. At the end of the sale, Dan asked Tom, "Why did you spend this money at my

---

4 Story adapted by Robert Wicks and found in his book *After 50*. The original story appeared in *The Last Word: A Treasury of Women's Quotes* by Carolyn Warner (Five Star Publications, reprint edition 2015).

store when you could have bought all of this stuff at a substantial savings at the big box store where you work?" Tom replied: "There is no one at the store who knows plumbing like you do. With the help you have given me, I think I can now do this job myself instead of calling a plumber."

In the nursing home, my mother had a habit of thanking a nurse or aide by saying "Thank you. I love you." One day an aide told me how miserable her home life was. "Your mother is the only person in my life who says I love you." My mother died fifteen years ago. Recently, I bumped into the aide, who said..."Your mother's kindness and love got me through the most difficult time in my life. I will never forget her."[5]

In our later years, we often have more time to focus on relationships—those we want to cultivate, rekindle, or repair. The Holy Spirit invites us to listen to the stirrings of our hearts in order to understand how we can best use our remaining time and energy to tend to our relationships.

FOR REFLECTION: *Are there people in your life, past or present, with whom you would like to rekindle a relationship? If so, how might you go about it?*

FOR READING: *John 15:11–17*

FOR LISTENING: *"One Spirit, One Church" (Kevin Keil and Maryanne Quinlivan, osu); "Anthem" (Tom Conry)*

---

5   Told to Sr. Janet Schaeffler, as found in her book *Let This Be the Time.*

30. The Gift You Are

In the ten years that I have been a spiritual director and the forty years prior to that, when I was a spiritual friend to dozens of people, I have repeatedly noticed a particularly disturbing characteristic. It seems that many people are unable to develop the kind of loving relationship with God that they crave, primarily because they think they are not worthy of it.

In their minds, they see themselves as flawed, sinful, simply not good enough to be deserving of a deep, loving relationship with the Lord. This is nothing short of a tragedy. While it is true that we are all flawed, all sinful, our relationship with God is not based on merit. We do not have to be perfect to develop a loving relationship with God. Thank God for that!

Although sacred Scripture and the teaching of the Church continually tell us that God's love for us is unconditional, many (if not most) Christians have an incredibly difficult time believing it. As a result, these individuals are unable to build a loving relationship with God that allows them to draw close, to feel God's embrace, and to see God as the ultimate cheerleader: always supporting us, always encouraging us, always communicating with us...always loving us.

I know that of which I speak. For many years, I had a form of obsessive compulsive disorder (OCD) called scrupulosity. The disorder caused me to focus on my brokenness, my sinfulness, and my unworthiness. For me, God seemed very distant, wanting to reach out to me, but hesitant—because I was simply not good enough. Gradually, as I received counseling, spiritual direction, and medication for anxiety, I came to understand that scrupulosity was the cause of these issues. As I began to believe in God's unconditional love for me, I began to feel God's profound presence in my life. I began to accept God's loving embrace. I began to understand that God's nature consists of all the wonderful traits of a loving father, a loving mother, and even a loving sibling, in the person of Jesus Christ: my divine brother, mentor, and friend.

There are a couple of reasons why I have waited until the final chapter to raise this topic. First, I wanted to give you a chance to get to know me by reading the other chapters in this book. Second, I want this chapter to be the final chapter that you read, in the hope that it will stick with you, that you will read it a second time, and that you will then go back and reread preceding chapters of this book with a revised perspective (if necessary) regarding who you are and how very much God loves you!

There is probably no greater message I can give you than the message that God loves you: NO MATTER WHAT! And I guarantee that once you are able to accept and embrace that message, and then act upon it, your life will never be the same. Your heart, soul, and mind will be different, and your life will take on a renewed vigor and a passion for God. You and I have been created in God's image and likeness, created from love to BE love. It is never too late to start! And God's abiding love will sustain us!

FOR REFLECTION: *When you are having difficulty feeling God's unconditional love for you, is there a close friend/confidant with whom you can share that? Is there anything you typically do to attempt to close the gap between you and God?*

FOR READING: *Romans 8:15–16; Romans 8:38–39*

FOR LISTENING: *"Shepherd Me, O God" (Marty Haugen); "The Center of My Life" (Paul Inwood); "All I Ask of You" (The Monks of Weston Priory)*

EPILOGUE

What will you leave behind?

Any series of reflections on spirituality and retirement must include the concept of legacy. It can be framed in various ways: What do I want to leave behind? How do I want to be remembered? What gift(s) do I want to give to the world? And so on.

The theoretically golden years of retirement are not always golden. In these years, many of us struggle with aches and pains and various physical and mental limitations that we must endure.

However, this does not mean we must abandon our desire to leave a legacy. In her book *Let This Be the Time*, Sr. Janet Schaeffler shares a poem written by a senior citizen who had read a story Sr. Janet had recounted about the famous violinist Itzhak Perlman. The poem speaks to several aspects of the retirement years, including the practice of leaving a legacy:

Itzhak Perlman broke a violin string
In the middle of a concert
The audience thought he would abort
But Itzhak signaled to the conductor
Nothing of the sort.

For six long minutes beautiful music
Came from his partially disabled violin
With just three strings Itzhak was able
To play every note therein.

As we grow old we must produce
With what's left within us—our best
Forget what we do not have
Make beautiful music with the rest.

Ideally, our retirement years provide ample opportunities to reflect upon what we have accomplished, not just in terms of career accolades but with regard to relationships with family and friends, volunteer activities, passing on the skills we have mastered, and defining the principles that have guided our decisions.

As part of our process of reflection, we can also ask ourselves such questions as these:

- Have I done what I would like to do in service to God's world—this amazing world in which I live?

- Is there still more I would like to do and can do?

- How do I want to be remembered?

A wise person once said: Whether or not we give much thought to our legacy while we are alive, it's a cinch that others will think about it after we are gone.

Some years ago, when I was a college campus minister, I asked the young adults attending our weekly gatherings to complete the following exercise: If you could write your own obituary, detailing how you would like to be remembered, what would it say? The responses were both fascinating and revealing. Some wrote about achieving career goals, some wrote of being loving spouses and parents, and so on. However, everyone wrote of personality qualities they hoped would be recognized by those whom they were leaving behind: descriptors such as loving, trusting, having integrity, being a person of faith, etc. Their responses demonstrated what was ultimately most important to them in that moment.

If you are so inclined, I invite you to take a few moments to complete this exercise yourself. Take a sheet of paper and draw a large tombstone on it. (I find this brings the exercise into sharper focus and helps the participant reflect at a more profound level.) Write your obituary on the tombstone. When you are finished, take the tombstone to prayer with the Lord. Don't expect any particular result; merely let the Holy Spirit guide your prayer.

And speaking of prayers, my prayer for you is that your retirement years will be filled with blessings that you can celebrate with others and with the Lord—and that God's peace will be with you.

Blessings and peace!
Bill

PLEASE VISIT MY WEBSITE:
www.findingspiritualdirection.com

BIBLIOGRAPHY

Anonymous, *How Can I Pray? (Daily Examen)*. Chicago: Loyola Press, 2017.
ignatianspirituality.com

Anonymous. "What Is Lectio Divina?" Rome: 2017.
http://ocarm.org/en/content/lectio/what-lectio-divina

Chittister, Joan. *The Gift of Years: Growing Older Gracefully*.
New York: BlueBridge/United Tribes Media Inc., 2007.

D'Arcy, Paula. "Presentation Given at River's Edge Retreat
and Conference Center." Cleveland, 2015.

Frankl, Viktor E. *Man's Search for Meaning*. Boston: Beacon Press, 2006.

Greenleaf, Robert K. *Servant Leadership: A Journey into the Nature
of Legitimate Power and Greatness*, 25th anniversary ed.
Mahwah, NJ: Paulist Press, 2002.

Miller, William B. *Finding Your Spiritual Direction as a Catechist:
Helpful Skills and Reflections for Personal Growth*. New London, CT:
Twenty-Third Publications, 2017.

Rohr, Richard. *Falling Upward: A Spirituality for the Two Halves of Life*.
San Francisco: Jossey-Bass/Wiley, 2011.

Ryan, Thomas. *Four Steps to Spiritual Freedom*.
Mahwah, NJ: Paulist Press, 2003.

Ryan, Thomas. *Soul Fire: Accessing Your Creativity*. Woodstock, VT:
SkyLight Paths Publishing/LongHill Partners, Inc., 2008.

Schaeffler, Janet. *Let This Be the Time: Spiritual Essentials for Life's Second
Act*. New London, CT: Twenty-Third Publications, 2020.

Wicks, Robert J. *After 50: Spiritually Embracing Your Own Wisdom Years*.
Mahwah, NJ: Paulist Press, 1997.